Richard Strauss

TONE POEMS: SERIES II

TILL EULENSPIEGELS LUSTIGE STREICHE

"ALSO SPRACH ZARATHUSTRA"

EIN HELDENLEBEN

in Full Orchestral Score

Dover Publications, Inc.

New York

Contents

This Dover edition, first published in 1979, is an unabridged and unaltered republication of the following three orchestral-score volumes:

Till Eulenspiegels lustige Streiche. Nach alter Schelmenweise—in Rondeauform—für grosses Orchester gesetzt von Richard Strauss. Op. 28, as published by the Jos. Aibl Verlag, Munich, ca. 1896 [first edition, later issue; first issue was 1895].
"Also sprach Zarathustra" / Tondichtung (frei nach Friedr. Nietzsche) für grosses Orchester von Richard Strauss / Op. 30, as published by the Jos. Aibl Verlag, Munich, 1896 [first edition].
Ein Heldenleben. Tondichtung für grosses Orchester von Richard Strauss. Op. 40, as published by the Verlag von F. E. C. Leuckart, Leipzig [1899; first edition].

New to the present edition are the full English translations of the German preliminary texts, instrumentations and composer's indications, specially prepared by Stanley Appelbaum. Considerations of space have necessitated the omission of the original German preliminary texts.

International Standard Book Number: 0-486-23755-9
Library of Congress Catalog Card Number: 78-68041

Manufactured in the United States of America
Dover Publications, Inc.
180 Varick Street
New York, N.Y. 10014

Seinem lieben Freunde
Dr. Arthur Seidl
gewidmet.

Till Eulenspiegels lustige Streiche.

Nach alter Schelmenweise - in Rondeauform -

für großes Orchester gesetzt von

Richard Strauß.

OP. 28.

Dedicated to his dear friend Dr. Arthur Seidl.

TILL EULENSPIEGEL'S MERRY PRANKS

Composed for Large Orchestra
After the Old Roguish Manner—in Rondo Form—
by
Richard Strauss.

Op. 28

INSTRUMENTATION: 16 first violins, 16 second violins, 12 violas, 12 cellos, 8 double basses. Piccolo, 3 flutes, 3 oboes, English horn, clarinet in D, 2 clarinets in B-flat, bass clarinet in B-flat, 3 bassoons, contrabassoon, 4 horns in F, 4 horns in D (ad libitum), 3 trumpets in F, 3 trumpets in D (ad libitum), 3 trombones, bass tuba. Timpani, triangle, cymbals, bass drum, snare drum, a large rattle.

GLOSSARY OF GERMAN PERFORMANCE INDICATIONS WITHIN THE SCORE

alle: all of them play; *allmählich lebhafter:* gradually more lively; *ausdrucksvoll:* expressively; *Becken allein:* cymbals alone; *Dämpfer weg:* remove mutes; *des:* of the; *des vorigen Zeitmasses:* of the foregoing tempo; *die eine Hälfte . . . die andere . . .:* one half . . ., the other . . .; *die Hälfte:* only half of them play; *die übrigen:* the others; *doppelt so langsam [schnell]:* twice as slow [fast]; *drängend:* urgently; *dreifach:* in three parts; *drohend:* threateningly; *dumpf:* muffled; *entstellt:* distorted; *erste Solovioline:* first solo violin; *Erstes Zeitmass:* first tempo; *etwas breiter:* somewhat more broadly; *etwas gemächlicher:* at a somewhat more comfortable tempo; *gedämpft:* muted; *Gemächlich:* comfortably paced; *geschmeidig:* with suppleness; *gestopft:* stopped notes; *geteilt:* divided; *gleichgültig:* with unconcern; *grosse Trommel allein:* bass drum alone; *im Zeitmass des Anfangs:* in the tempo of the beginning; *immer (ausgelassener und) lebhafter:* more and more (exuberant and) lively; *Immer sehr lebhaft:* continuing very lively; *kläglich:* mournfully; *lang:* long; *leichtfertig:* frivolously; *liebeglühend:* amorously; *lustig:* merrily; *mit Dämpfern:* with mutes; *mit Holzschlägel(n):* with (a) wooden stick(s); *mit Schwammschlägeln:* with soft sticks; *nicht eilen!:* don't rush!; *nicht geteilt:* not divided; *offen:* open notes; *ohne Dämpfer:* without mutes; *ruhig(er):* (more) calmly; *Saite:* string; *scharf gestossen:* with sharp staccato; *schelmisch:* roguishly; *schnell und schattenhaft:* fast and shadowy; *sehr lebhaft:* very lively; *Solobratsche:* solo viola; *steigern:* more intensely; *vierfach:* in four parts; *Volles Zeitmass:* full tempo; *wieder noch einmal so langsam:* just that much slower again; *wütend:* furiously; *zart:* tenderly; *zusamm(en):* together; *zweite Soloviolinen:* second solo violins.

Till Eulenspiegels lustige Streiche.

Richard Strauss, Op. 28.

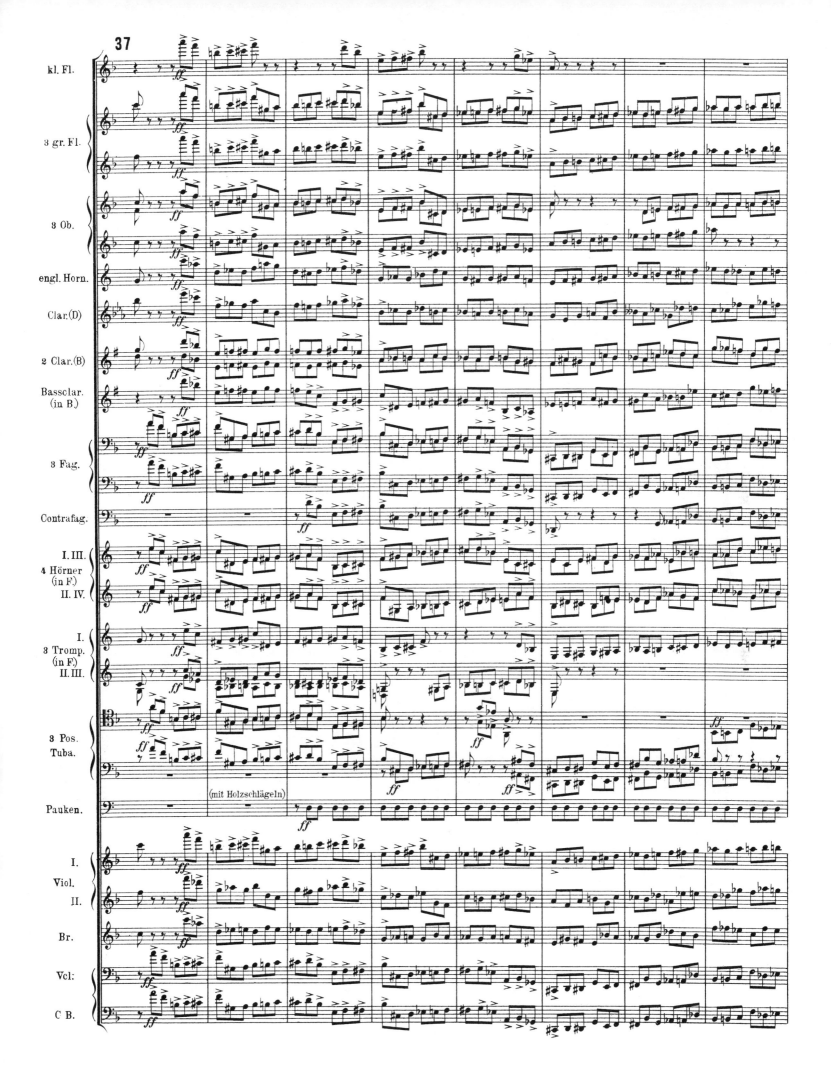

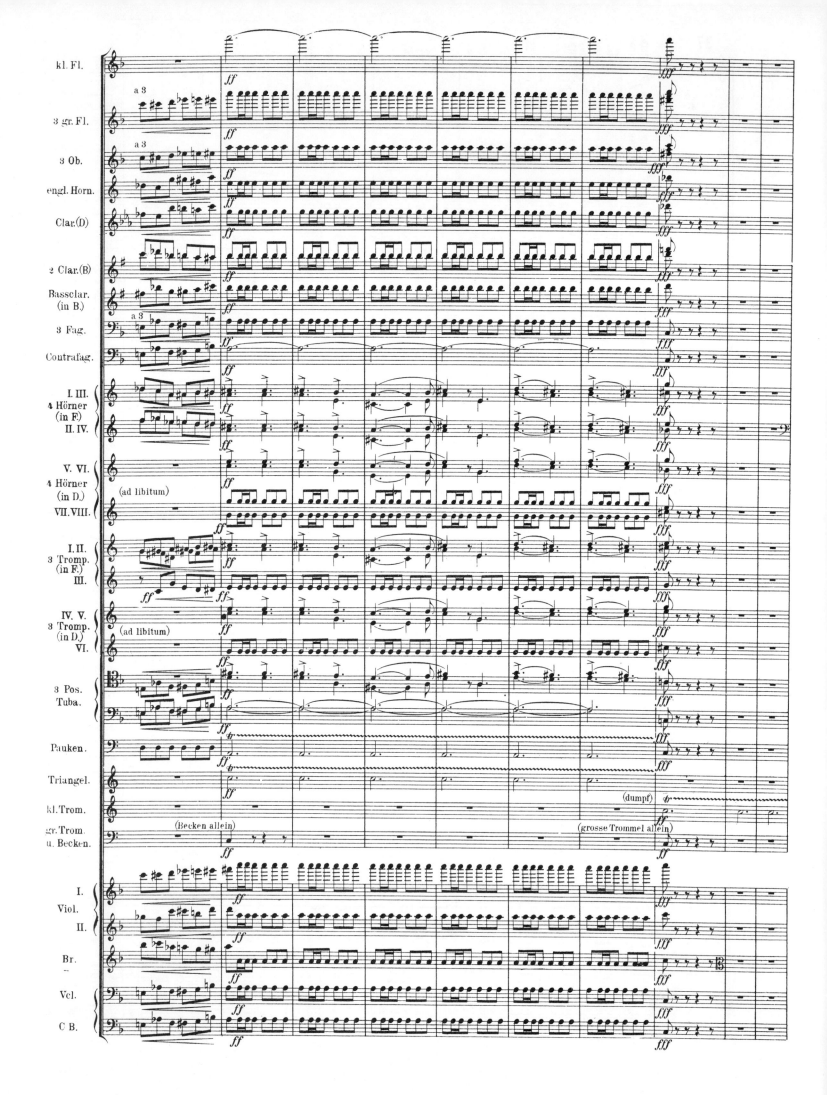

Epilog.

Doppelt so langsam. (im Zeitmass des Anfangs ⁴⁄₈)

München, 6. Mai 1895.

"Also sprach Zarathustra"

Tondichtung

(frei nach Friedr. Nietzsche)

FÜR GROSSES ORCHESTER

von

Richard Strauss

OP. 30.

"THUS SPAKE ZARATHUSTRA"
TONE POEM

(freely based on Friedrich Nietzsche)

for Large Orchestra
by
Richard Strauss
Op. 30.

ZARATHUSTRA'S PREAMBLE (by Nietzsche)

When Zarathustra was thirty years old, he left his homeland and the lake of his homeland and went up into the mountains. Here he enjoyed his intelligence and his solitude and did not weary of them for ten years. Finally, however, his heart was changed—and one morning he arose with the dawn, stepped before the sun and addressed it thus:

"You mighty star! What happiness would be yours if you did not have those for whom you shine? For ten years you have been coming up here to my cave: you would have been sated with your light and this path if it were not for me, my eagle and my serpent.

"But we awaited you each morning, took your overabundance from you and blessed you for it.

"Behold! I am tired of my wisdom, like a bee that has gathered too much honey; I have need of outstretched hands.

"I want to give and distribute gifts until the wise ones among mankind have once again grown happy in their folly, and the poor in their wealth.

"For that purpose I must descend into the deep: as you do in the evening when you go beneath the sea and bring light to the underworld, you abounding star!

"I must, like you, be submerged, or 'perish,' as those men say to whom I wish to descend. So bless me, you calm eye, who can look upon even far too great good fortune without envy.

"Bless the goblet that wants to run over, so that the water flows from it in a golden stream and bears the reflection of your rapture everywhere!

"Behold! This goblet wants to become empty again, and Zarathustra wants to become a human being again."

— Thus began Zarathustra's descent.

INSTRUMENTATION. STRINGS: 16 first violins, 16 second violins, 12 violas, 12 cellos, 8 double basses, 2 harps. WOODWINDS & BRASS: piccolo, 3 flutes (the 3rd player doubles as 2nd piccolo), 3 oboes, English horn, E-flat clarinet, 2 B-flat clarinets, bass clarinet (in B-flat), 3 bassoons, contrabassoon, 6 horns, 4 trumpets, 3 trombones, 2 bass tubas. ORGAN. PERCUSSION: timpani, bass drum, cymbals, triangle. Orchestral bells, a deep bell 𝄢

TRANSLATION OF SECTION TITLES WITHIN THE SCORE. *Page 65:* "Of Those at the Back of the World." *Page 70:* "Of the Great Longing." *Page 75:* "Of Joys and Passions." *Page 85:* "The Dirge." *Page 92:* "Of Science." *Page 100:* "The Convalescent." *Page 124:* "The Dance Song." *Page 167:* "The Song of Those Who Come Later."

TRANSLATION OF FOOTNOTES. *Page 66:* The organ should be very faintly sounded, so that it acts as an accompaniment throughout and the strings take the lead. *Page 96:* All violins spiccato! *Page 175:* Begun February 4, completed August 24, 1896; Munich.

GLOSSARY OF GERMAN PERFORMANCE INDICATIONS WITHIN THE SCORE

alle: all of them play; *allein:* alone; *alle Violonc. mit springenden Bogen:* all cellos spiccato; *allmählich etwas bewegter:* gradually more agitated; *allmählich etwas weniger langsam:* gradually less slowly; *allmählich wieder bewegter:* gradually more agitated again; *am Steg:* at the bridge; *ausdrucksvoll:* expressively; *aushalten:* prolong the note; *B:* B-flat; *Becken mit Holzschlägel:* cymbals with a wooden stick; *bedeutungsvoll:* with significance; *Bewegt(er):* (more) agitated; *breiter werden:* play more broadly; *Dämpfer weg:* remove mute; *des:* of the; *. . . des vorigen Zeitmasses:* . . . of the foregoing tempo; *die Hälfte:* half of them play; *die übrigen:* the others (the rest); *doppelt so schnell:* twice as fast; *dreifach:* in three parts; *energisch:* energetically; *ermattend:* growing weary; *erste:* first; *etwas beruhigend:* calming down somewhat; *etwas breiter werden:* somewhat more broadly; *etwas lebhafter:* somewhat more lively; *etwas ruhiger:* somewhat more calmly; *etwas weniger langsam:* somewhat less slowly; *etwas zurückhaltend:* holding back somewhat; *feierlich:* solemnly; *Festes Zeitmass:* steady tempo; *früheres Zeitmass:* earlier tempo; *gestopft:* stopped notes; *get(h)eilt:* divided; *gewöhnlich:* resume normal mode of playing; *harpegg(irt):* arpeggio; *heftig:* violently; *hervortretend:* prominently; *immer bewegter:* more and more agitated; *immer breiter:* more and more broadly; *immer langsamer:* more and more slowly; *immer mehr beschleunigen:* speed up more and more; *immer mehr steigern:* more and more intensely;

immer ruhiger: more and more calmly; *immer schneller:* faster and faster; *im Zeitmass:* in tempo; *klagend:* lamentingly; *leicht schwebend:* lightly floating; *leicht und elastisch:* lightly and elastically; *Mässig langsam, mit Andacht:* moderately slow, with reverence; *mit Dämpfer(n):* with mute(s); *mit Holzschlägel:* with a wooden stick; *mit Humor:* humorously; *mit lebhaftem Schwung:* with lively zest; *mit lebhafter Steigerung:* with lively intensity; *mit Paukenschlägeln:* with timpani sticks: *mit Schwung:* with zest; *nicht get(h)eilt:* not divided; *noch bewegter, sehr leidenschaftlich:* even more agitated, very passionately; *noch langsamer:* even more slowly; *offen:* open notes; *ohne Dämpfer:* without mute; *ohno Solovioline:* without solo violin; *Pult:* desk; *pultweise geteilt:* divided by desks; *Saite:* string; *sehr ausdrucksvoll:* very expressively; *Sehr bewegt:* with great agitation; *Sehr breit:* very broadly; *sehr feurig:* very ardently; *sehr heftig:* very violently; *sehr langsam:* very slowly; *sehr lebhaft und schwungvoll:* very spiritedly and energetically; *sehr schnell:* very fast; *Solovioline:* solo violin; *vierfach:* in four parts; *volles Werk:* full organ; *von hier ab fest in Zeitmass:* from this point on, at a steady tempo; *weniger breit:* less broadly; *zart ausdrucksvoll:* with tender expression; *zart bewegt:* with tender movement; *Ziemlich langsam (in Vierteln):* fairly slowly (in quarter beats); *zusammen:* together.

„Also sprach Zarathustra!"

Tondichtung (frei nach Friedr. Nietzsche)
für grosses Orchester.

Richard Strauss, Op. 30.

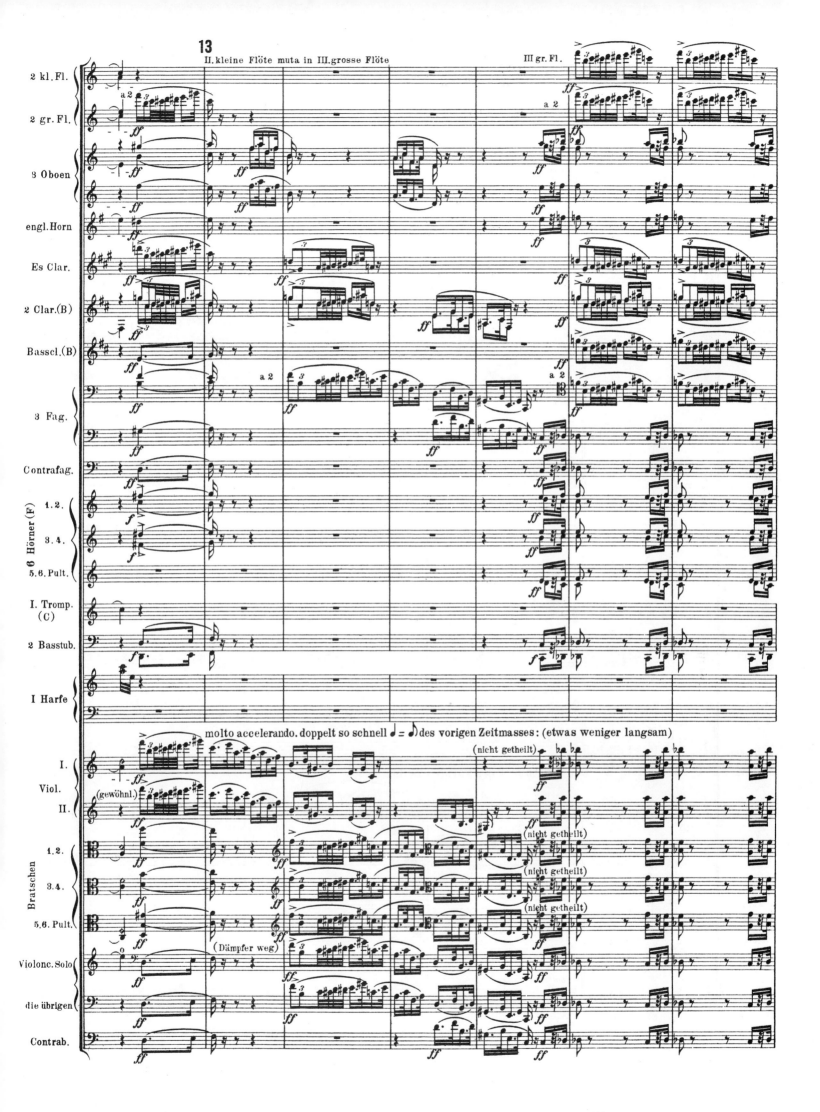

immer bewegter.

(etwas beruhigend)

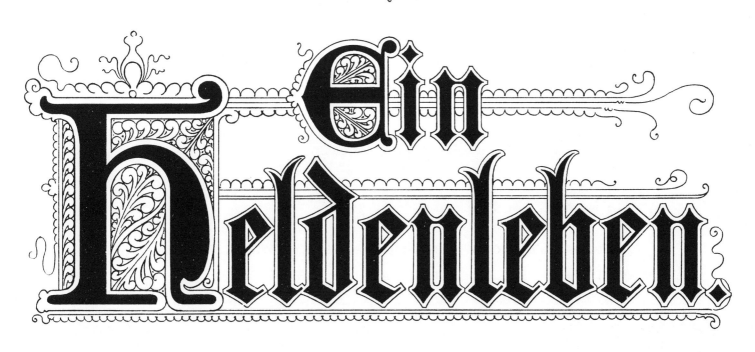

Ein Heldenleben.

Tondichtung für großes Orchester

von

Richard Strauss.

Op. 40. Partitur. Pr. netto M 36,—

A Hero's Life

TONE POEM FOR LARGE ORCHESTRA
by
Richard Strauss.

Op. 40.

NOTE: We have retained the standard translation "A Hero's Life," but a truer version would be "A Heroic Life." "A Hero's Life" would correspond to *Das Leben eines Helden* or *Eines Helden Leben*.

INSTRUMENTATION

WOODWINDS: piccolo, 3 flutes, 3 oboes, English horn (also doubles as 4th oboe), E-flat clarinet, 2 B-flat clarinets, bass clarinet, 3 bassoons, contrabassoon.
BRASS: 8 horns, 5 trumpets, 3 trombones, tenor tuba in B-flat, bass tuba.
STRINGS: 16 first violins, 16 second violins, 12 violas, 12 cellos, 8 double basses, 2 harps.
PERCUSSION: timpani, bass drum, cymbals, small snare drum, large tenor drum.

TRANSLATION OF FOOTNOTES. *Page 210:* ⁓ indicates portamento between tones. *Page 220:* ⁓⁓⁓ always means pronounced portamento! *Page 258:* Spiccato.

GLOSSARY OF GERMAN PERFORMANCE INDICATIONS WITHIN THE SCORE

alle: all of them play; *alle übrigen:* all the rest; *allmählich etwas fliessender:* gradually more flowing; *allmählich immer ruhiger:* growing gradually calmer; *allmählich im Zeitmass etwas steigern:* quicken the tempo gradually; *allmählich nachlassen:* slacken gradually; *allmählich wieder lebhafter:* gradually more lively again; *ausdrucksvoll:* expressively; *aushalten!!:* prolong the note!!; *Becken gewöhnlich:* cymbals played the usual way; *beinahe doppelt so langsam (schnell):* nearly twice as slowly (fast); *beruhigend:* calming down; *. . . bis—fest im gewonnenen, lebhaften Zeitmass:* until attaining a lively tempo, then steady; *Dämpfer weg:* remove mute; *. . . des vorigen Zeitmasses: . . .* of the foregoing tempo; *die Hälfte:* half of them play; *die übrigen:* the others (the rest); *doppelt so schnell:* twice as fast; *drängend (und immer heftiger):* with urgency (and more and more violently); *dreifach:* in three parts; *Erstes Zeitmass:* first tempo; *Es:* E-flat; *etwas breit(er):* somewhat (more) broadly; *Etwas langsamer:* somewhat more slowly; *etwas markirt:* somewhat marcato; *Festes Zeitmass:* steady tempo; *gedämpft:* muted; *gestopft:* stopped notes; *Ges wieder nach G umstimmen:* tune G-flat back to G again; *geteilt (pultweise):* divided (by desks); *getragen:* sustained; *G nach Ges herunterstimmen:* tune G down to G-flat; *Heftig bewegt:* with violent agitation; *hervortretend:* prominently; *heuchlerisch schmachtend:* hypocritically languishing; *hinter der Scene:* offstage; *hoch:* high; *immer langsamer:* more and more slowly; *immer ruhiger:* more and more calmly; *immer schneller und rasender:* more and more rapidly and wildly; *im Orchester:* in the orchestra; *im Zeitmass:* in tempo; *kräftig, heiter:* powerfully, humorously; *lange Pause:* long rest; *Langsam:* slowly; *lebhaft:* lively; *Lebhaft bewegt:* with lively motion; *leicht beschwingt:* lightly soaring; *leichtfertig:* frivolously; *liebenswürdig:* amiably; *lustig:* merrily; *Mässig langsam:* moderately slowly; *mit Dämpfer(n):* with mute(s); *mit grossem Schwung (und Begeisterung):* with great zest (and enthusiasm); *mit Holzschlägel(n):* with (a) wooden stick(s); *mit Steigerung:* with intensification; *nicht abdämpfen:* do not mute; *nicht geteilt:* not divided; *ohne Dämpfer:* without mute; *plötzlich wieder ruhig und sehr gefühlvoll:* suddenly calm again and very affectionate; *Pult:* desk; *Saite:* string; *schnarrend:* rasping; *schnell und keifend:* fast and naggingly; *sehr ausdrucksvoll:* very expressively; *sehr energisch:* very energetically; *sehr getragen:* very sustained; *sehr lebhaft:* very lively; *sehr ruhig:* very calmly; *sehr scharf (und spitzig):* very sharply (and pointedly); *Solobratsche:* solo viola; *Soloviol[ine]:* solo violin; *spielend:* playfully; *träumend:* dreamily; *übermütig:* in high spirits; *viel bewegter:* much more agitatedly; *viel lebhafter:* much more lively; *viel ruhiger:* much more calmly; *vierfach:* in four parts; *voll Sehnsucht:* full of longing; *vom 1. Pult:* from the first desk; *weich:* gently; *Wieder (etwas) langsamer (ruhiger):* (somewhat) more slowly (calmly) again; *wieder lebhaft:* lively again; *wieder sehr ruhig:* very calmly again; *wie ganz von ferne:* as if from a great distance; *zart(,) ausdrucksvoll:* with tender expression; *zart, etwas sentimental:* tenderly, somewhat sentimentally; *zart hervortretend:* tenderly standing out; *zart und liebevoll:* tenderly and lovingly; *ziemlich lebhaft:* fairly lively; *zischend:* hissing; *zornig:* angrily; *zurückhaltend:* holding back; *zweifach:* in two parts.

Ein Heldenleben

Richard Strauss, Op. 40.

21
fest im gewonnenen, lebhaften Zeitmass.
kl. Fl.
dim.
I.
3 gr. Fl.
II.III.
dim.
3 Oboen.
engl. Horn.
Clar. (Es)
2 Clar. (B)
BasscIar. (B)
3 Fag.
f sfz
6 Hör. (F)
III. IV.
V. VI.
VII. VIII.
2 Tromp. (Es)
3 Posaunen.
(ohne Dämpfer)
fest im gewonnenen, lebhaften Zeitmass.
21
I.
Violinen.
II.
f sehr energisch
(Dämpfer weg)
cresc.
Bratschen.
Violonc.
Contrab.

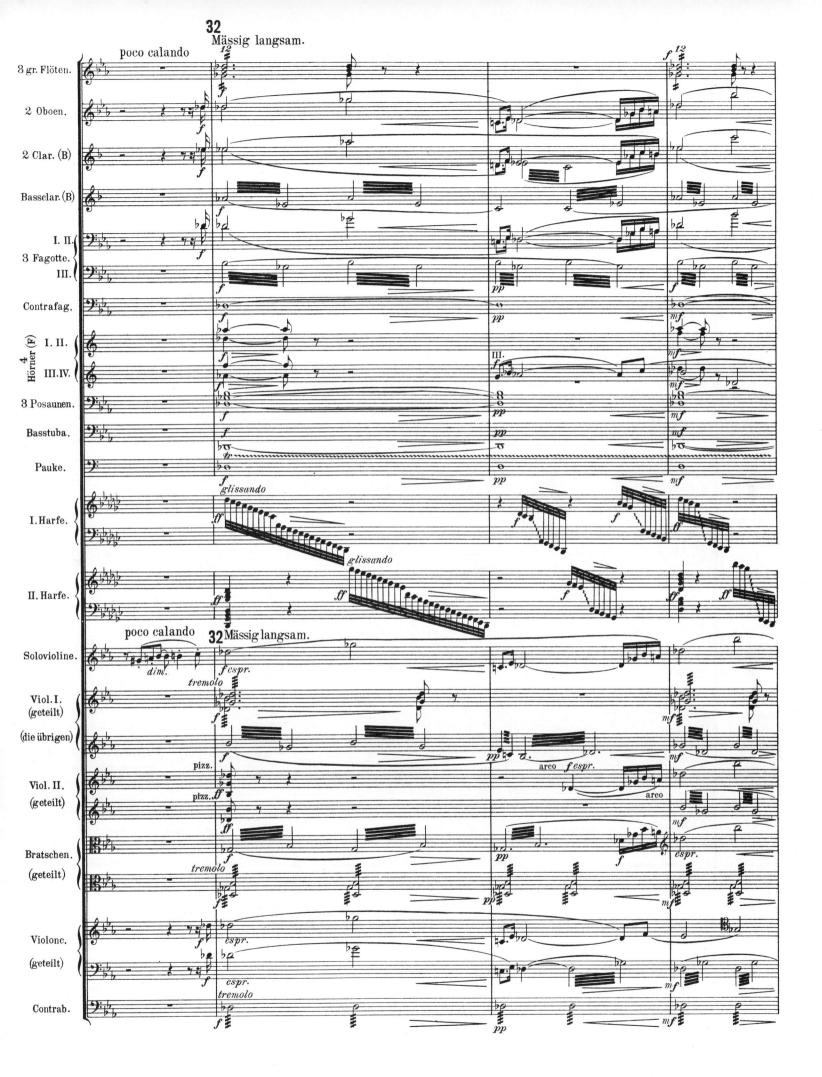

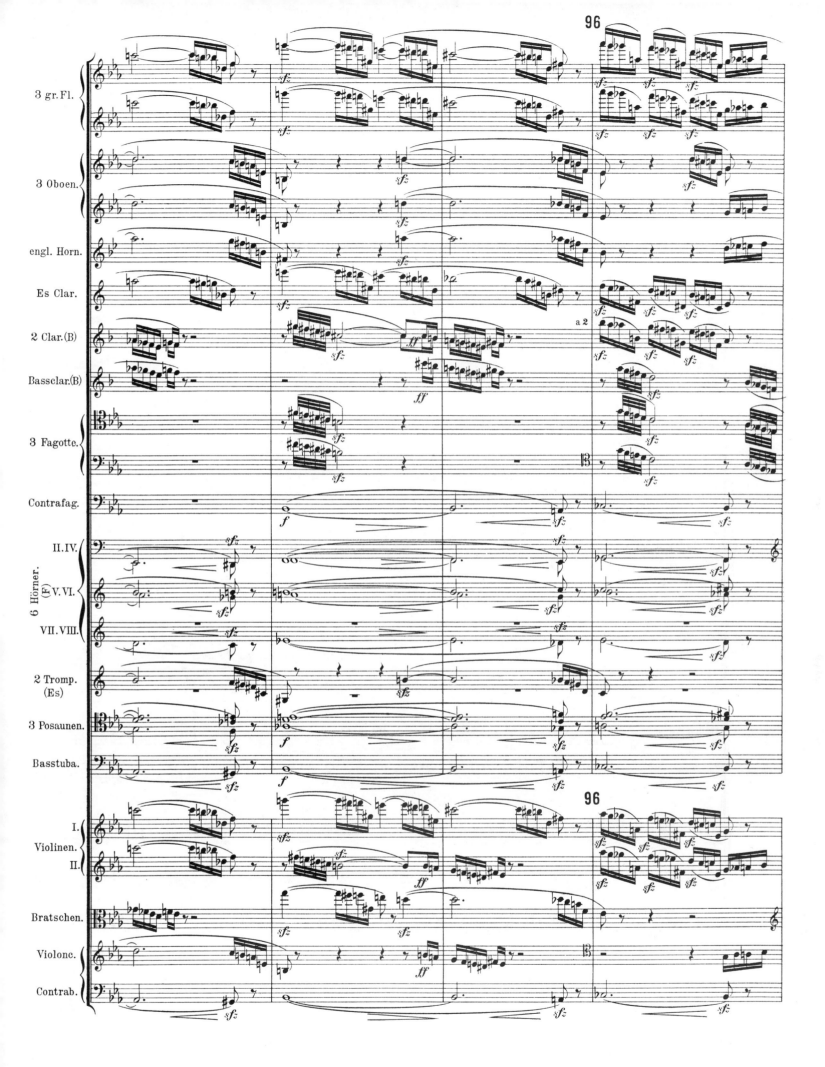